Mozart

C000128541

Wise Publications
London/New York/Paris/Sydney/
Copenhagen/Madrid

MUSIC·LINK
£ 4.95

Exclusive Distributors:
Music Sales Limited
8/9 Frith Street, London W1V 5TZ, England.
Music Sales Pty Limited
120 Rothschild Avenue, Rosebery, NSW 2018, Australia.

This book © Copyright 1993 by
Wise Publications
Order No. AM91043
ISBN 0-7119-3367-7

Music processed by Interactive Sciences Limited, Gloucester
Book design by Hutton Staniford
Music arranged by Stephen Duro
Compiled by Peter Evans

Photographs courtesy of:
London Features International

Music Sales' complete catalogue lists thousands of titles and is free from your local music shop,
or direct from Music Sales Limited. Please send a cheque/postal order for £1.50 for postage to:
Music Sales Limited, Newmarket Road, Bury St. Edmunds, Suffolk IP33 3YB.

Theme from Symphony in G Minor

K.550

With movement

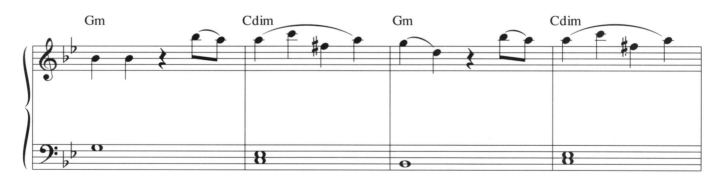

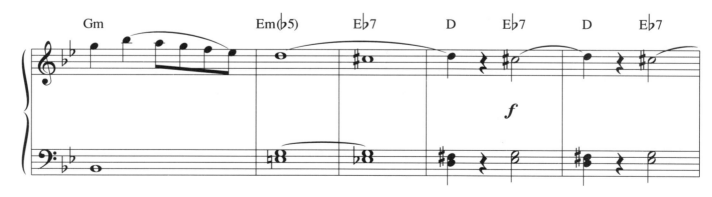

Theme from Piano Concerto in C Major (Elvira Madigan)
K.467

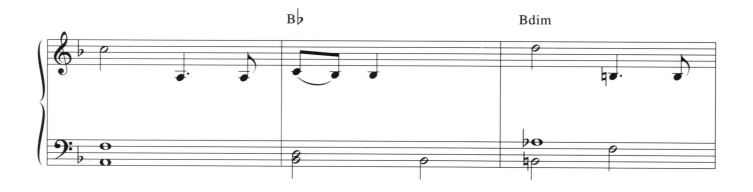

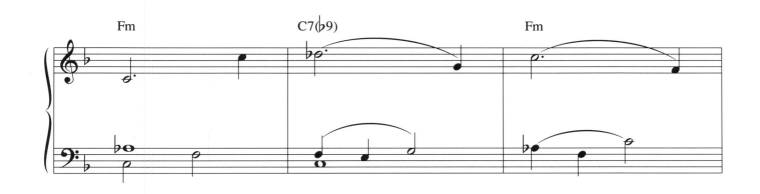

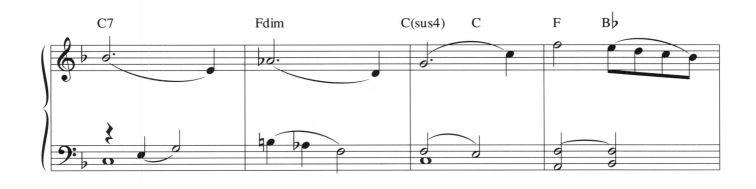

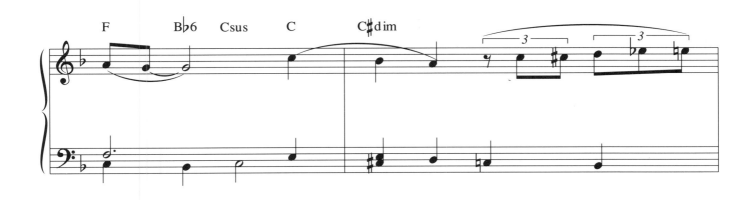

1st Movement Theme from Eine Kleine Nachtmusik

K.525

Romance from
Eine Kleine Nachtmusik
K.525

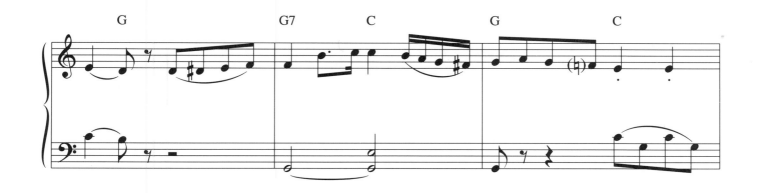

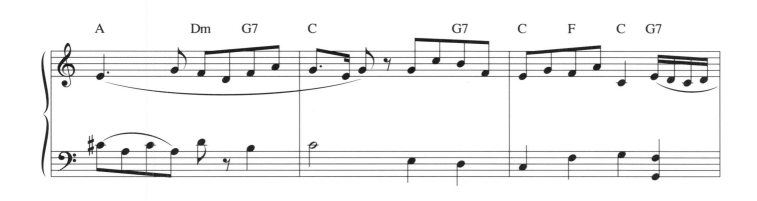

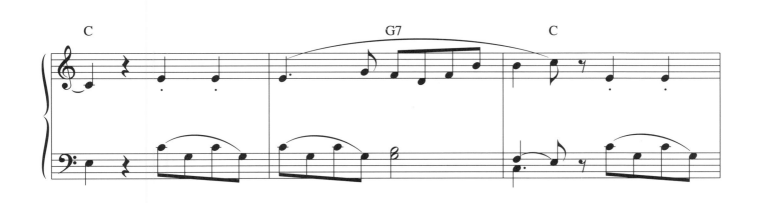

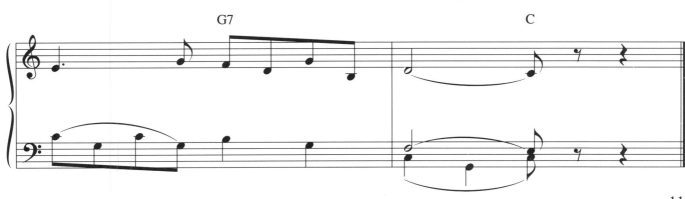

Minuetto from
Eine Kleine Nachtmusik
K.525

With movement

13

Rondo Theme from
Violin Concerto in D Major
K.211

Minuetto Theme from Haffner Symphony
K.385

Moderately

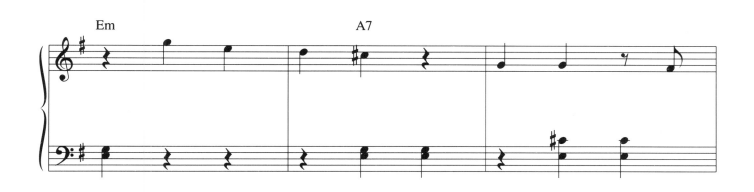

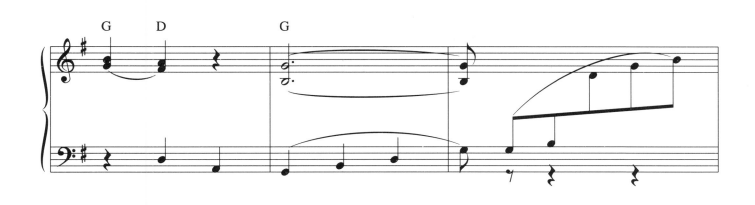

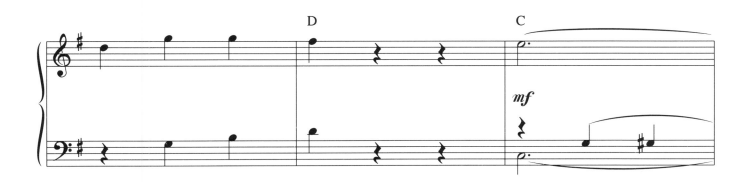

Ave Verum Corpus

19

O Isis And Osiris
From The Magic Flute

Rondo Alla Turca
From Sonata in A
K.300

With movement

The Manly Heart
That Claims Our Duty
From The Magic Flute

March Of The Priests
From The Magic Flute

Say Goodbye Now To Pastime
From The Marriage Of Figaro

Bright

Tell Me Fair Ladies
From The Marriage Of Figaro

Moderately

Minuet in F
K.2

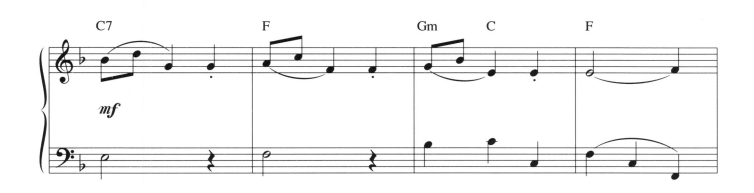

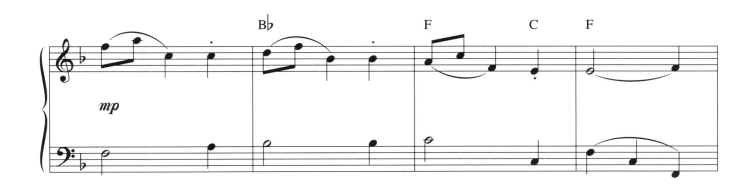

Minuet from Sonata in E♭
K.189

Last Movement Theme from
Sonata in C Minor

K.456

2nd Movement Theme from
Sonata in C

K.545

1st Movement Theme from
Sonata in A
K.300

Moderately

Song: "To Friendship"

Slow Movement from
Piano Concerto in B♭
K.450

Là Ci Darem La Mano
(You'll Lay Your Hand In Mine)
From Don Giovanni

poco rit.

44

Last Movement Theme from Violin & Piano Sonata in E♭

K.481

With movement

Slow Movement Theme from Violin & Piano Sonata in C
K.296

Moderately

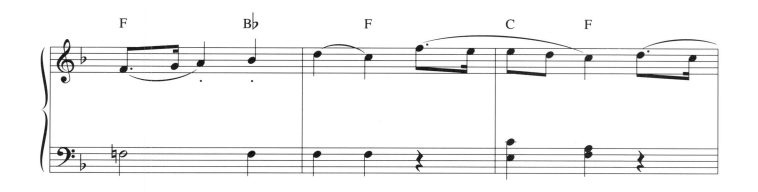

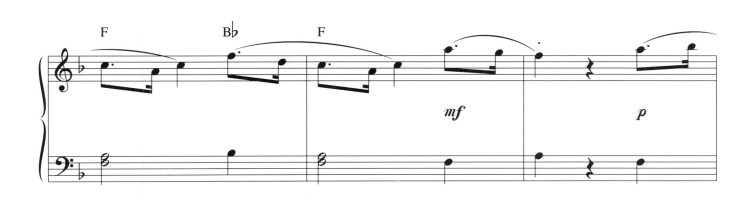

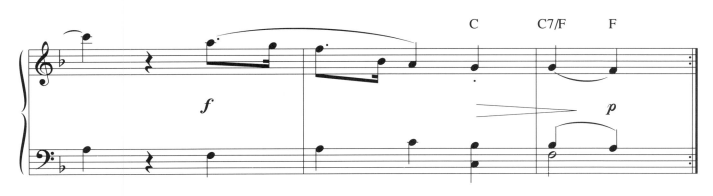

Song: "Lullaby"

1/94 (16906)